CW00327964

KENILW ANCIENT TRACKS

Thoughts and Notes on the Evolution of
the Road System in the
Kenilworth Area.
A Thesis based on evidence found
on the ground.

Robert J. Steward

ODIBOURNE PRESS
KENILWORTH 1997

KENILWORTH'S ANCIENT TRACKS

Acknowledgements:
John Drew, *Yesterday's Town* (1980)
Harry Sunley, *A Kenilworth Chronology* (1989)
Steven Wallsgrove, *Kenilworth 1086-1756* (1991)

Office colleague (ch. 1) : James Yuill
Irene Potter : notes by

Warwickshire County Record Office
Archaeology Field Office, Warwick

Maps and photographs by the author
Printed by B.J.T. Print Services Limited
ISBN 0 9515147 9 2

Contents

MAPS

FOREWORD

Much has been said in the past about mythical 'Ley Lines' but not really about 'Old Straight Tracks' as Alfred Watkins discovered and wrote about in the 1920s. His theory has been rejected by some historians as being unsupported and valueless.

I refute these allegations and show that by studying the positions of odd lengths of road, large stones, old bridges, fords, excavations and archaeological finds, together with the geology and topography, the alignment of ancient tracks and the formation of later road systems can be found.

My theory has been arrived at from first principles. By that I mean it is based purely on what I have seen on the ground. The study of the relationship of one feature to another reveals an amazing amount of further information. By taking fording places and bridges, for example, and a little patience in aligning them intelligently careful thought reveals in some cases interesting phenomena which are not coincidental.

It has been made totally independent of any writings on the subject. It was not until the sequence of events had been established as I believed, that I referred to documents from 1086 onwards to verify my theory. I was pleased to find that the documentation provided proof in most cases, and I was able to make corrections and additions in others. All through I have based my theory on hard facts.

The analysis of such things can be accomplished in a village or town where the building of suburbia has not yet taken place and where much of the pre-20th century still remains.

Here in Kenilworth I have undertaken and produced what I believe to be the forming of the road system in this area from the end of the last Ice Age up until the end of the 18th century, answering some of the questions regarding roads which have puzzled historians and showing possible reasons why certain things are where they are.

These thoughts should give historians something to ponder about. Even if my theory is proved wrong, it may help to lead to the right solution of the system of tracks, their direction and the main places they linked together for trade, security, etc., in ancient times.

Some of the ancient tracks did not reveal themselves until working on the 17th and 18th century period. The Stoneleigh Road in Stoneleigh is one such example.

During the period covered by this book the metric system did not exist in England, but in this present metric age I have given heights and distances in that system followed by the equivalent English units in brackets. However, because short distances were generally measured in 'feet' and 'rods' (a rod = $16\frac{1}{2}$ feet) I found it prudent to reverse the order in Chapter 11 and place English units first, following by metric in brackets.

1. PRE-ROMAN

Ever since I was a small boy of six or seven years old I have been fascinated by the possibility of straight ancient tracks. My father had brought home from our local library Alfred Watkins' **The Old Straight Track** which had been published two or three years before. We looked through it together. In Norfolk, where we lived, I only knew of one and that was 'The Peddars Way'.

Coming to live in Kenilworth in 1959, my interest was aroused again as I saw the possibilities of straight ancient tracks here in the Midland Counties. I had been given a copy of Watkins' book, and was discussing it with an office colleague who told me that he noticed an alignment from 'The Mount' on Ryknild Street at Beoley eastwards along various Parkland drives into my area. I investigated it eastwards where it finished up at Gibbet Hill on Watling Street a total distance of 48 km. (30 miles) in a straight line!

I was thus prompted to make further observations, and in this first chapter I have written down the findings on which I was able to base my conclusions.

******

In the triangle formed by the old Roman roads, Ryknild Street in the west, Fosse Way in the east and Watling Street in the north, there appears to be a number of alignments which must date back to Neolithic times.

Taking an area about Kenilworth there are seven which seem to be fairly probable, of which one seems certain. The seven referred to I have named A,B,C,H,K,L and M (the missing letters refer to alignments in other parts of the country).

'LINE A' goes from the MOUNT at Beoley, on Ryknild Street in the west to GIBBET HILL on Watling Street in the east.

'LINE B' follows a line from Rubery church along odd lengths of road such as Table Oak Lane, through a MARK STONE on the Birmingham Road within the Kenilworth boundary to Crackley Bridge over the stream at Milburn Grange.

'LINE K'. This seems to have been an important alignment running west from The Salt Way by the river at Droitwich. It crosses Ryknild Street just south of MOONS MOAT, Redditch, through Baginton and if carried on, it passes through Peterborough to Castle Acre on the Peddars Way in Norfolk. It crosses Crackley Bridge at Kenilworth at which 'LINE B' probably finished.

'LINE L'. Between Forhill on Ryknild Street and Eathorpe on the Fosse Way. But it probably actually only went from the Fosse Way to where it met 'LINE K'

5

'LINE H'. From the Rugby direction over Stoneleigh Bridge where it met 'Line L' at the fording point over Inchford Brook, Kenilworth.

'LINE M'. This alignment does not tie up with any of the aforementioned lines. Whereas the others generally lie east-west, this is north-south. It follows the main road through Balsall Common in a southeast direction, a slight kink, and then straight on in a south easterly direction over Victoria Bridge at Leamington Spa.

These alignments make interesting following when read in conjunction with geographical and physical features. High points and river crossings play a large part, as do the contours of the sloping ground and valleys. In the Kenilworth area with which we are concerned here the levels range from 46m (150ft) above O.D. to 130m (425ft), a range of just 84m (275ft).

The Finham Brook catchment area, which consists of all Kenilworth plus a little way beyond northwards and southwest, drains into the River Sowe, and almost immediately into the River Avon, covers approximately 36 sq. km and lies in a shallow bowl with the odd area of higher ground.

At the west side of this bowl, where a number of streams meet, the land tends to be boggy, draining east into a channel of lower ground which is the valley of the Finham Brook.

An area of 10km east-west by 7km north-south with the 36sq. km 'bowl' in the middle is the area which concerns us here. But to go into more detail with the alignments, the area outside our 10 x 7km area must be looked at.

Firstly, look at 'LINE K'. In the west from Droitwich, the alignment crosses Ryknild Street and passes just south of MOONS MOAT, an area of lake dwellers. Through HAY WOOD at Baddesley Clinton, recorded to be one of the oldest woods in the area, it follows the position and direction of an existing track through this wood. Its course from the old Keeper's Lodge towards Abbey Farm seems to suggest it has been there for a very long time. In Honiley it passes close to, but just south of, a moat and by the side of ST. JOHN'S WELL, over the footbridge at the south-west corner of Chase Wood and diagonally across the wood and over the BRIDGE in Chase Lane spanning Finham Brook. Carrying on over CRACKLEY BRIDGE on the Coventry Road picking up and following the general direction of the road past Wainbody Farm, between Stoneleigh Road and Kings Hill, and on into BAGINTON. From there it meets the Fosse Way at BRETFORD, fording the River Swift at Cosford and eventually joining Watling Street near TRIPONTIUM. Between Bretford and King's Newnham there is a Neolithic settlement where there are ring ditches and a cursor-like earthwork; flint flakes and bronze artifacts have been found there.

Working back westwards, at Baginton the Romans had a fort and the Saxons a graveyard. At a point just 180m. (200yds) south of the line a Neolithic axe was unearthed in 1939. Rowley Road follows this line as well to Tollbar End. This is a new road, put through to replace the old road destroyed by the building of the air strip. However, there was a track and footpath along part of the line of Rowley Road before 1900, as shown on O.S. maps of that date.

The road past Wainbody Farm has already been mentioned; about 135m (150 yds) from where it meets Stoneleigh Road along the line towards Crackley Bridge another axe head was found in 1934.

From Baginton westwards the ground rises from 61m (200ft) at the River Sowe, falling at each water course, until it reaches 122m (400ft) at St. John's Well. The crossing of water courses every 2 or 3km would be welcomed watering places for travellers on foot. At a number of these stream crossings there are now bridges on the line or very close to it.

Returning to Crackley Bridge, once over the stream coming from Baginton there is a branch going a few degrees north of west, this is my 'LINE B'. As previously said, this line heads for Rubery church. Just inside the Kenilworth boundary on a north-south ridge is a MARK STONE just beside the present Kenilworth to Balsall Common Road. This 'Mark stone' gives the direction to aim for as you leave the stream crossing at Crackley. (There must have been other stones along the route, but these have long since gone.) Table Oak Lane follows the line and just past is a moat on its south side, and a short length of road 1.5km further on. There are other points which seem to be significant. Extending Table Oak Lane eastwards shows a track of about 180m (200yds) long which leads to a pond. Remains of a sighting pond perhaps?

At first there seemed to be evidence that this alignment carried on eastwards from Crackley Bridge to the Bronze Age site near Ryton Wood. But I cannot find any evidence of a crossing of the River Sowe on this line, apart from a footbridge shown on a 1/25000 O.S. map 100m (110yds) down stream, and nothing where it crosses Finham Brook or the Avon. This does not mean, however, there were no crossings at these points.

Let us now investigate 'LINE L'. I noticed that the BOUNDARY STONE at the north-east corner of the erstwhile Fernhill Wood by a stream at the junction of the Kenilworth, Honiley and Beausale c.p.'s boundaries lines up with a footbridge across the Inchford Brook, and the MILESTONE in Warwick Road, Kenilworth opposite Moorlands Avenue. Extending the line westwards, the alignment passes through the 'Y' junction at Baddesley Clinton. But at 2.3km west from the Boundary Stone before reaching Baddesley Clinton it joins 'LINE K' on a ridge near the highest point in the area of 130m (425ft), and about 0.6km west along 'LINE K' from St. John's Well. Eastwards from the Boundary Stone, after crossing Inchford Brook, another stream is crossed before coming to the

Milestone in Warwick Road, then over the Avon by Ashow Church where a footbridge is still extant. Passing through Stonehouse Farm and then 10.5km on to Eathorpe where it crosses the River Leam about 100m up stream of the present bridge. Perhaps the 100m error could be accepted in early man's efforts of survey, on the other hand the crossing could have moved down stream with time and erosion to its present spot.

In the area we are considering, working westwards, our alignment 'LINE L' runs along fairly level ground rising and falling no more than about 15m (50ft) for 1.3km to the River Avon and then rises to a little over 15m (50ft) in 1km, from the Avon at 45m (150ft) O.D. to cross the saddle formed by two small hills of 76m (250ft) plus. It then falls slightly and again rises to a higher plane of undulating ground of 76 to 84m (250 to 275ft) on which Kenilworth now stands. In the first of the valleys we find the Mile Stone. Incidentally following along this particular valley is Warwick Road. The next valley has the stream alongside Brookside Avenue. The third and last accommodates Inchford Brook. This area is very marshy and was once included in the 'Great Lake' between the early 13th century and c.1649 A.D. Here 'LINE L' crosses the Inchford Brook at 76m (250ft) and rises very steadily at first, through the Boundary Stone at 84m (275ft) and steeply to 130m (425ft) to meet alignment 'LINE K'.

'LINE H' we will next look at. It branches off from 'LINE L' where it crosses Inchford Brook, in an easterly direction towards Stoneleigh where it crosses the River Sowe by the bridge there. Leaving Inchford Brook in a marshy area, the land rises about 8m (25ft) then drops down 15m (50ft) to the stream at the foot of Forrest Road at 69m (225ft) O.D. by the BORROW WELL, and up the hill to 91m (300ft) where the War Memorial now stands, and on to Leyes Lane whose full length aligns with 'LINE H'. It passes through a corner of the eastern part of the Kenilworth boundary, which suggests there may have been a 'mark stone' here at sometime. It then crosses the River Sowe at Stoneleigh Bridge and straight up the hill and on.

The undulations on this 'LINE H' are not more than 8m (25ft) once the 15m (50ft) level of the Avon valley has been left. There is just the 90m (300ft) high hill at Abbey End, which stands up dead on line. It appears that our ancient surveyors left the fording point on the Inchford Brook, and made a 'bee line' for this hill 50ft higher than they were, then carried on in the same straight line fording the River Sowe, and straight up the other side.

We now have what appears to be a main ancient trackway running north-east by east to south-west by west, through Kenilworth, 'LINE K'. At Crackley Bridge, after crossing the stream we have a branch off going north-west by west, 'LINE B'. Further along at Honiley, on a high point, another track branches off south-east by east, which itself, after crossing Inchford Brook, has a branch off to the north-east by east. It is well to note here that branching off from one track to another occurs at river crossings or high points.

There is what appears to be evidence of two other alignments. Firstly 'LINE M' lies north-west to south-east. The alignment of the road through Balsall Common, from the cross roads at the centre to the junction with Meer End Lane, and projected onwards crosses Chase Lane, Kenilworth, at a point where each side of the lane a hedge coincides with the line for a total distance of about 1km. Projecting the line even further southwards it crosses the River Leam at Leamington Spa at Victoria Bridge, crossing the Cattle Brook on route at the existing crossing on the Warwick Road near Leek Wootton.

The second of these two alignments, which I have designated 'LINE A', joins Ryknild Street at the MOUNT at Beoley, with GIBBET HILL on Watling Street, catching the north part of Kenilworth in the middle of its length. It follows the Drive through Umberslade Park, Packwood House and its Avenue and causeway with the ponds each side of it, along an average line of the zig-zag of the Kenilworth boundary into Kenilworth and across the upper reaches of Finham Brook at a small stone-arch bridge. It runs through Stoneymoor Wood, where I found and photographed in 1980 evidence of a 'hollow way' on the alignment. A boundary point where, until Dutch Elm disease killed it, an old elm tree once stood is on the line and nearby, also on the line a good size pond, followed by another boundary point at the corner of Broadwells Wood. Thence across a stream where Gibbet Hill Road bridges it and through a moat between the Coventry Road and the railway line. The next few kilometres pass through an area where all evidence has been destroyed, but it emerges again alongside the south edge part of Birchley Wood.

The next notable point on 'LINE A' is the Moat at Harborough Magna, and the road to Churchover which follows the line to the River Swift where there is a ford, and here again the present ford is downstream by less than 100m. There is an 'S' bend in the river here, and it can easily be understood how the fording point would move downstream. In just under three km Watling Street is reached at Gibbet Hill, a junction of three other roads. The altitude of this hill is 131m (430ft), the Mount at Beoley at the western end is 138m (450ft) high. A straight line between these two high points is 48km, that is 30 miles.

There is, however, a deviation in this line which at the centre runs north of a dead straight line by about 67m (73yds) which is 1 in 361 or $4^3/_4$ yards per mile. This is calculated from the O.S. grid, which, bear in mind, is a flat grid on a curved surface. No allowance has been made for this difference. However, if there is an error of only 67m (73yds) at the centre and return to their objective again, it shows the skill achieved by these early surveyors. As mentioned earlier, these two last alignments, 'A' and 'M', do not appear to have any connection whatsoever with the alignments 'B', 'H', 'K' and 'L', which suggests they are of a different era, whether later or earlier it is difficult to determine. The fact that so much of 'LINE A' survives and a small stone-arch bridge exists over the upper reaches of Finham Brook in the middle of a field, makes the later date more probable, or at least it was still in use until much later if it was an earlier one.

'LINES B' and 'M' intersect at a Kenilworth boundary point, with 'LINE A' passing 91m (100yds) north. Could this be significant?

I mention boundary points along some of these alignments. When boundaries were established, existing geographical features were used. Rivers and streams were a common feature, and so were existing large stones, which in many cases were standing stones or mark stones. Another example of this is on the alignment I call 'LINE D' which runs parallel to part of the Fosse Way. It is the Four Shire Stone, near Moreton-in-Marsh, aligning with a standing stone and a fallen (?) stone. This 19th century 'stone' at the junction of four shires is no doubt a replacement of a much earlier standing stone.

Looking at the 'Roman Roads', it is found they usually run from high point to high point or river crossing or a saddle between two hills before changing direction. For example, take a length of the Fosse Way. Moving south from Leicester, it runs straight from the centre of the city for 19km, crossing the River Soar at an altitude of 73m (240ft) on its way, to HIGH CROSS where it crosses another Roman Road, Watling Street at an altitude of 134m (440ft). It then runs in a slightly different direction, but nevertheless straight, for 12km to the River Avon where it again changes direction. Incidentally here is another case of a river crossing shifting downstream over the ages. From here it goes straight for 7km to cross the River Leam near Eathorpe, continuing for 28km to the bridge over the River Stour at Halford; it is almost a complete straight line. It first goes straight for 19km to a hill at Compton Verney at a height of 116m (380ft), and then a slight change of direction to Halford. This causes a deflection of about 200m off a dead straight line.

This gives some idea of how these Roman Roads lie, and in many cases were based on existing ancient tracks at the time.

It is easy to see how to go in a straight line from hill to hill where it is possible to see your destination, or from a low point to a hill, but how did they go from one low point, such as a river crossing, to another in a straight line? Presumably they aimed in the direction they wanted to go, and went until they came to a river and crossed it at that point. Streams were easily forded, but rivers? Did they build smokey bonfires to aim for where a crossing was possible? Whatever method they used, their sense of direction was very much better than anyone has to-day. A directional sense akin to animals, which man has lost through lack of full use over the millennia since these alignments were made.

For whatever reason they were made, be it for religious reasons to travel to religious places a long distance away, or for trading purposes, it seems there must have been a general command that these alignments should be made, particularly the very long distance ones. Was it by the command of religious orders?

It is quite clear to me that the Romans used some of these alignments as a guide or actually took them over and put them to good use in their own road network, extending them, perhaps, in some places, or building parallel to suit their own military requirements.

Were the alignments made by an early society put to use as track ways by a later society who were themselves predecessors of the Romans? The whole subject is full of questions.

As mentioned earlier, the Fosse Way crosses the alignment, my 'LINE D', 4km south of Moreton-in-Marsh, then changes direction following south-west and parallel to, but 2km south-east of, 'LINE D' which aligns FOUR SHIRE STONE near Moreton with the 'HOAR STONE', a standing stone near Lower Swell, and 'HANGMAN'S STONE', a flat stone near Yanworth. This 'LINE D' passes through or very close to at least four churches, Yanworth, Turkdean, Cold Aston and Upper Slaughter, and also with the 19th cent. Great Wolford Church built in the confines of early earthworks. But what is also significant is the forded river crossing, now with a bridge by its side at Upper Slaughter, indicating it was a trackway. It looks as though the Romans ignored the existing track route and built their own road parallel to it, or had the ancient track become unusable by then?

The finding of two Neolithic axe heads on 'LINE K', one at Baginton and the other about 3km further west, shows that Neolithic man went this way. They might have been lost while cutting the way through forest which covered most of this area long ago. On the other hand, the two axes found here, and others at Canley and Lapworth are from Caenarvonshire, and could have been lost by traders. Carried by dug-out canoe down the River Severn to Droitwich, they could have been unloaded there for distribution down The Salt Way and along 'LINE K' to the east.

'MOONS MOAT', near Redditch, where 'LINE K' passes a little south, was a lake dwelling site of around 5,000 B.C. Projecting the line in the eastern direction, it passes through Peterborough and low-lying ground where more lake dwellings have been found. Then on to meet the Peddars Way in Norfolk at Castle Acre. There is no proof, however, that it ever went so far. A few hundred yards, or metres, south of 'LINE K' is the marsh land west of Kenilworth Castle. Crossing this marsh is 'LINE M', with 'LINES L' and 'H' close by. Was this area once the site of lake dwellings?

It is not the object of these notes to discuss by whom, exactly when or why these alignments were made, apart from saying that the evidence found on the ground makes me believe they were trackways and they were probably made around 4,500 B.C. for the purpose of trading and journeying to religious gatherings.

No mention has yet been made of 'LINE C'. Projecting a line from the southern end of Crackley Lane, it aligns with the diagonal footpath across Abbey Fields and through 'Goodrest'. Twenty six km (sixteen miles) further south it passes through the west edge of the FORT on MEON HILL. If carried on it intersects a number of crossroads and aligns with a couple of short farm tracks. In the northern direction it aligns with a high point of 91m (300ft) at Canley. 12.5km further on it passes through Griff on the Bedworth-Nuneaton Road where there is believed to have been a 'Neolithic axe factory'. Then in another 7.5km it meets a hill of 107m (350ft) on top of which Higham-on-the-Hill sits at 1km north of Watling Street.

The Line 'Stoneleigh Bridge to Westley Bridge and on to Cryfield Grange', appeared as I was investigating ENGLISH LANE. This would have been only a minor alignment, as is 'LINE X' which aligns Glasshouse Lane with the existing footbridge between Ashow and Bericote over the River Avon.

In the above, only major alignments have been discussed. There were, of course, other less important tracks in existence, not necessarily straight. One is that which follows the north-west bank of the River Avon from Finham to Warwick. On its way it passes around the foot of BLACKLOW HILL where in 1972 excavations yielded up a Saxon site and Mesolithic arrow heads. Another was a trackway from the 'War Memorial' on the intersection of 'LINES C' and H' southwards crossing 'LINE L' at the Mile Stone in Warwick road, and continuing on to cross the River Avon at Chesford Bridge after crossing the Finham to Warwick Track. Over the river it made for Offchurch. This became the drovers' road down from Wales.

2. THE LAST ICE AGE

In the last chapter I touched on the subject of Lake Dwellers. Going back 70,000 years to the last ice age, we find Kenilworth lies only about two or three miles from the western shore and half way up the last ice age lake, Lake Harrison. Edge Hill was part of the southern shore line, the northern shore line was just above Leicester and the eastern shore line was just east of Daventry. The level of the lake would probably have been around the 91-122m (374-400ft) contour mark. A few miles west of where Coventry now stands was an island on which Corley now sits at its southern end at an altitude of 180m (590ft).

The last ice age lasted 10,000 years and up to this time the water had drained north into the Trent and then the North Sea. When the climate warmed up the Severn Valley ice to the south melted first, the water of Lake Harrison broke through, washing away the soft deposited material on the lake floor, thereby hollowing out the south-flowing Avon valley.

For some long time the bed of the now defunct Lake Harrison remained wet, but gradually dried up in the higher areas. There seems, however, to have been a pocket where it took a very long time to dry out, for even today that area still tends to be marshy. The area in question is that bounded by Honiley in the west, Chase Lane in the north, Warwick Road in the east and the curve of Rouncil Lane in the south.

Rouncil Lane follows the higher and drier land around this area, which up to probably 5,000 B.C. was a lake surrounded by a bog. Rouncil Lane then may be a descendant of an old Mesolithic track which circled around the south side of this area, keeping to the dry ground above the 84m (275ft) contour, except for two places, at the ford through the Inchford Brook and at Woodcote Lodge. It may even have been a branch off the track following the north bank of the River Avon down to the Mesolithic site at Blacklow Hill.

Neolithic Man, around 4,500 B.C. making his straight tracks trading in axes and salt, could have decided that here in Kenilworth was a likely place for a lake dwelling. To my knowledge no excavations have ever taken place in this area to disprove this thought.

The present gap between the Castle and higher ground to the south may not have existed then and the whole area bounded by the 79m (260ft) contour was a lake. Tracks A, B, C, K, W and X could have existed. Then after the water of the lake broke through by the Castle and progressively wore the channel, the level of the lake gradually drained to more or less as it is today, allowing tracks H, L and M to be made.

The Roman sites in Kenilworth are all on or above the 84m (275ft) contour line. Crew Farm and Glasshouse wood are at this level while Cherry Orchard and Chase Wood sites are at 91m (300ft). This seems to suggest that 2,000 years ago in Roman times, land below the 84m (275ft) contour was still unsuitable for habitation, although crossing it was possible.

The mark stones in this area are also on or above this level. The mark stone, now the mile stone in Warwick Road, is only about a metre below. It may be significant that the axe head found on "Track K" where it crosses "Track Y" is at the 84m (275ft) contour.

Another interesting thing worthy of note is that *'the way through the fields'* shown on James Fish's map 1692 also keeps just above the 84m (275ft) contour. Clinton Lane is below, showing that it was cut after the level of the marsh fell.

The woods around the 'Neolithic Lake' above the Castle are and were above the 84m (275ft) contour level, that includes Thornton Wood. There are woods below this level in other parts of Kenilworth and Stoneleigh along the Avon Valley, where the water probably drained away quicker and the land tended to be less marshy.

This may also explain why there is no evidence of Roman occupation around the old village of Kenilworth. The land there is all below 84m (275ft) and where it is above, the ground is steep. It probably was not habitable until early Saxon times.

3. THE ROMANS

When the Romans invaded this island in 43 A.D. their first objective was to subdue the inhabitants by building fortifications in strategic places connected by good lines of communication.

As any army would do, the Roman army used the good routes already existing and selected ones would have been improved from the narrow earth tracks they probably were into wide paved roads. Others perhaps were left as they were.

At Baginton they built a fort near an ancient trackway. It was situated about 15m (50ft) above the River Sowe which surrounds it on the north, west and south, and by the River Avon on the east and south-east. The only approach to it without a crossing a river was from the north-east from the Fosse Way at Bretford along the prehistoric 'Line K'. A look at the map will show existing roads which follow this general line.

Having established themselves, the Romans, to make their stay more permanent, searched for materials for building, such as clay for making roof and floor tiles and for making pottery. Their search for suitable clay took them among other places to 'Cherry Orchard' and 'Chase Wood'.

Their route to 'Cherry Orchard' I believe, with little doubt, would have been along the existing, at that time, "Track K", as I now call it, fording the stream where Crackley Bridge now is, then bearing left over the higher ground through the Common, down to Finham Brook to ford it at Mill End. The track from Common Lane to the fording point still exists. By following the little stream, on the south side of Finham Brook towards its source, a gentle climb brought them to the 'Cherry Orchard' site. The 'Chase wood' site could have been found from "Track K" as it is only about 200m off the track to the south.

In time a way of joining the two sites was found along Finham Brook's north bank. This route was from the ford at Mill End, keeping to the higher ground as the valley of the Brook would be marshy, and along what we now call Lower Ladye's Hill. Then following the dry ground roughly along where Pears Close now is into Abbey Fields, along the top of the bank on which the Priory was later built, continuing on between the Abbey Gate House and the 'Barn'. The track then followed the top of the bank where a row of some very old oak trees still grows, to Castle Green and down Purlieu Lane. The existing footpath south of Chase Wood follows the old Roman track, meeting "Track K" again just before a foot bridge and St. John's Well.

It is quite possible that for travelling from the 'Cherry Orchard' site to the 'Chase Wood' site a short-cut was sought without having to back-track to Mill End. This route may have been along the present Spring Lane, crossing the small stream there on the way. Then making for and fording Finham Brook, a little east of Townpool Bridge at an existing fording place on 'Line C' to join their North Bank track, and on to the 'Chase Wood' site down Purlieu Lane. This is total surmise, of course. A look at a map showing contours and water courses only, will help to get the picture.

As 'Cherry Orchard' was only 100m from "Track H" the Romans may have also used this ancient route to the 'Chase Wood' site, as there was a well on the way. By going from the BORROW WELL in an almost direct line to the North Bank track they would cross the little brook, not where the bridge is now, but in a straight line at a point 137m (450ft) north of the present bridge to ford Finham Brook at the FORD. A large scale map shows that Borrowell Lane aligns with the Ford. Then continuing up more or less as it does now to meet their North Bank track, and westwards down Purlieu Lane etc. This route kept the crossing of marshy ground to a minimum.

There may well have been an ancient trackway existing from the Ford northwards, which the Romans used to meet their North Bank track. This track, whenever made, ran directly from the Ford up a shallow valley through the present 'Queen and Castle' car park, keeping to the higher ground to the west of a little stream coming down from 'Bull Hill'. It met the ancient "Track K" at the east end of Chase Lane. This length of track, from the 'Queen and Castle' to "Track K" is called on the 1692 James Fish map *the way through the fields*. It then followed the east bank of the small tributary of Finham Brook to Burton Green, the old line of Red Lane. The Kenilworth boundary was formed on the east side of this track. The line of *the way through the fields* where it met "Track K" and carried on north, can be seen by the hedge line and trees at the junction of Beehive Hill and the Birmingham Road.

At the bottom of Red Lane the old hedge line, which followed the east side of the old track up to Burton Green, can still be seen behind the spinney on the corner with the Birmingham Road. It lines up with the east bank of the stream on whose east bank the track followed. (An electric switchgear housing now stands over it!) At this same point a track was formed crossing this small tributary from the west to join it. (*See* chapter on The Drovers).

In time, the new way through the Common and along the north bank of Finham Brook would have been used more than the part of "Track K" between Crackley Bridge and St. John's Well. That length of track would have gradually fallen into decay, as it had not been 'paved'. Similarly, lengths of "Tracks B, H and L" became unused. The crossing points of the streams and short lengths of track remained because of use by the local inhabitants.

At Lapworth, at a little under 1km south of "Track K", is another Roman kiln

16

site. It is also only a few metres north of another probable alignment 'Line W'. 'Line W' aligns the boundary stone on the corner of Fernhill Wood on 'Line L', with Haseley Knob cross roads, the main drive through Wroxhall Abbey, one km of road at Rowington Green, a road junction at Liveridge Hill (a hill of 165m. 542ft), and meeting Ryknild Street at a cross roads at Ipsley Court at an altitude of 93m (340ft) to continue to Headless Cross.

Following closely to the north-east of Crew Lane runs the remains of an ancient 'hollow way'. Excavations carried out for the by-pass in 1977 showed it was later used by the Romans by being repaired in their style. Romano-British occupation was also discovered at Crew Farm in that area, which it will be seen is only a few metres off 'Line H'. The north-west end of this 'hollow way' has been lost to the golf course. I believe the existing road from Knowle Hill down to Finham Brook is the extreme north-west end of the track. It has been found that the 'hollow way' carries on in the other direction down to the River Avon.

A straight line taken from the west end of Crackley Bridge to Ashow footbridge, near the church, passes along the line of Glasshouse Lane from the Lodge at Glasshouse Wood to Knowle Hill. It picks up the old 'hollow way', mentioned above, at the top of Knowle Hill. Was this another ancient track? I have called it 'Line X'. A Roman Villa has been found in Glasshouse Wood. An old pathway along the south bank of Finham Brook probably existed from 'Line C' to the crossing of Finham Brook at Finham and was used by the Romans. Most of it still exists. The length of road from Westley Bridge to Finham does not now exist. It is shown, however, on Thos. Jeffrey's map of 1752 and on Thos. Kitchin's map of 1760. By 1793 it had gone, as Wm. Yates' map of that date does not show it. The trackway from Finham Bridge southwards leading to Warwick by keeping to the west of the River Avon, in Norman times was known as 'Warwic Wey'. The present Warwick Road out of Kenilworth did not exist at that time, except perhaps in the form of an animal track.

In their search for materials, the Romans may have been enticed up a small shallow valley just north of the fording point of Finham Brook at 'Line C'. This is Fieldgate Lane and Hollis Lane. I found a piece of Roman grey ware in a field close to 'Line A'. There is evidence at the junction with Beehive Hill that Fieldgate Lane ran straight into Hollis Lane. The hedgerow shows this to be so. The present divergence happened much later when Beehive Hill was constructed in *c*.1756.

The Romans left in 411 A.D., having made their mark on England after 400 years of occupation.

4. THE WELSH DROVERS

I believe it was during the Roman occupation that the drovers began to move large quantities of cattle from Wales to the south of England. This mass of cattle continued to be driven until the advent of the railways in the nineteenth century.

Many of the Welsh drovers followed the route through Balsall Common and Kenilworth along the Welsh Road.

Through Kenilworth they may have first driven their cattle down "Track M" to the marshy ground in the Inchford Brook basin to be watered, turned east towards the hill on which the Castle now stands, then along Purlieu Lane to cross the Ford using part of the Roman track (or did the Romans use the drovers' track?). From the Ford onwards to meet "Track H" at the 'Borrow Well', around the bottom of the hill to meet Warwick Road instead of up "Track H" to the 'War Memorial' and down the south-east side to Warwick Road and on to the Welsh Road.

Some drovers may have come down from Burton Green along Red Lane, Birmingham Road and '*the way through the fields*', meeting other drovers at the Ford.

Those drovers using "Track M" later may have turned east when they met "Track B", meeting the drovers coming down Red Lane, thus avoiding the marsh, which by this time may have become impassable. In time short cuts were taken. The 'mark stone' on "Track B" could be seen from the 122m (400ft) ridge on "Track M". From this high point they made for the mark stone, picking up a short length of "Track B", and made their way southwards keeping to the south of the hill, but up from Finham Brook, until they came to the little stream which they crossed at the bottom of Red Lane, joining the track leading to the Ford.

With the increase in cattle traffic and because of the marsh, "Track M" inside the present Kenilworth boundary went out of use, as far as droving was concerned, and all traffic went down through '*the way through the fields*'. No doubt the inhabitants of that area objected to this mass of cattle tramping through their allotted land. The '*way through the fields*' kept above the 84m (275ft) contour, that is above the marsh level at that time. (*See* Chapter 2). Later, when the marsh level receded, a diversion was made lower down towards the brook, now called Clinton Lane. Incidentally, could all those cattle coming up Purlieu Lane have worn it into the 'valley' it is today especially during wet weather by churning up the mud?

From where it crosses a corner of the boundary from the north-west into Kenilworth "Track M" in half a km, cuts close between 'North Chase Farm' House 200m to the south-west and 'Chase Farm' 100m to the north-east. Farmers on the routes of the drovers were only too pleased to graze the cattle that passed their way, as it was an excellent and cheap way to fertilize their fields. Could it be these two farms owe their existence to such an enterprise?

The hedge line on "Track M" where it crosses Chase Lane seems to suggest that the track was in existence until quite late. Part of the west edge of Thornton Wood ran along it, giving the impression it existed up to the eleventh century in some form. It seems, too, that Rudfin Lane did not come into existence until the drovers began to come through that way, leaving suspicions of "Track M" to the present day. The enclosing of the Chase area in the twelfth century also must have helped in the obliteration of "Track M". The short cuts involving "Track B" would soon have put that length of "Track B" from "Track M" to Crackley Bridge out of use.

I imagine after the Romans had abandoned 'Cherry Orchard', "Track H" went out of use between there and the 'Borrow Well'. The rest, apart from Leyes Lane and the bridges, had dwindled away long before.

In his book, **The Drovers**, K.J. Bonser says Neolithic Men were drovers and if this is so, the Romans could have used the Neolithic crossings at the Ford and the track up to the 'Borrow Well', also making use of Purlieu Lane.

As suggested earlier, there was not the need for large movements of cattle before the Romans came. The demand did not arise until the Roman occupation when there became large concentrations of people in the towns and cities they created.

Looking west along the line of the "Roman Way" from Bridge Street. The village of Chinewrda would have been on the right.

19

5. THE SAXONS

After the Romans the Saxons, a more agricultural race, were the next to leave any real mark on the English countryside up to the Norman Conquest. By Domesday in 1086, the track system had altered, but leaving traces of the ancient track alignments and Roman roadways.

It seems that "Track L" had gone, leaving only mark stones and fording points. "Track H" had disappeared apart from a length, now Leyes Lane, the crossing of the River Sowe at Stoneleigh together with a length of track up the hill and the Borrow Well in Kenilworth. Ancient "Track K" had dwindled in the area under consideration to a 1.5km straight length east of Stoneleigh Road to Hill, a two hundred metre length at Crackley Bridge, the crossing over Finham Brook in Chase Lane and the south-west corner of Chase Woods. Ancient "Track B" just had left Table Oak Lane and about two hundred metres outside 'Redfern Manor' where the 'mark stone' exists. "Track C" had partially survived north of the War Memorial and, albeit in a much modified form even to this day, in the Warwick direction through 'Goodrest'. This modification is not surprising as that area tends to be marshy and was also 'enclosed'. This 'way' and that following the west side of the River Avon were the roads between Warwick and Kenilworth and Warwick and Coventry. "Track M" gradually became redundant, as mentioned in the chapter on the Welsh Drovers, just two or three km at Balsall Common and the crossing of Cattle Brook, which survived because of local use. (The Warwick Road did not exist then.)

Was the way to Coventry via "Track C"? The alignment in the northerly direction heads for Canley, crossing alignment "A" on the Gibbet Hill Road at the bridge over the little stream. Although alignment "A" crosses the stream near enough at right angles, "Track C" runs nearly parallel to the stream, passing close on the west of 'Cryfield Grange'. The fact that in 1154 a petition to the King was made by the Cistercian Hermits of Cryfield complaining about the noise made by travellers on the highway disturbing their prayers, confirms that this very well could have been the way to Coventry in those days and that "Line C" did exist as a "Trackway".

As farmsteads were established, access to them came off existing trackways, gradually, in time, altering direction to suit locations and to shorten the distance. This could be why Chase Lane moved off "Track K" to its present position to serve farms around the hamlet of Blackwell.

The possible reason for the location of the early settlement of Kenilworth was the crossing of the stream at that point and the intersection of two busy ways. Like so many other towns it was established at a river crossing with an intersecting road running along one or perhaps both banks of the river. The north-south way crossed Finham Brook and the east-west way was along the north bank of the Brook.

The small community would have favoured the region on the north bank, which is the south-facing side of the Finham Brook valley. It would be drier and sunnier, with the roadway and brook in front of them to the south.

In the time of the Saxons there would have been small timber dwellings in the area where St. Nicholas' Church and the old Kenilworth Hall now stand.

The Roman track from 'Cherry Orchard' to Townpool Bridge went out of use, except for what is now Spring Lane and the crossing of the stream at its lower end. Extant possibly, as mentioned before, because of local use.

This is, I suggest, how the Kenilworth or 'Chinewrda' road or way system looked in 1086. Since then there have been further changes.

The avenue of trees planted in the early 1900's along the line of the "Roman Way". 'Barn' to the left, 'Gatehouse' to the right.

21

6. THE FOUNDING OF THE PRIORY
c. 1124

The Augustinian monks were given land in Kenilworth by Geoffrey de Clinton to build a priory. In the south the land was bounded by a line which went from the top of the hill, on which the War Memorial now stands, in an easterly direction along the hill generally parallel to Finham Brook. Here it met the eastern boundary at some geographical or boundary point existing at the time. The eastern boundary then joined up with a point a little east of the present traffic lights, via the crossing of Finham Brook, which was to the east of the present Townpool Bridge and to which line the row of 16th-17th century cottages, still existing, was built.

This act cut off the villagers' ancient diagonal way down to Finham Brook crossing along "Track C". A detour had to be made. This became Abbey Hill on the south and Rosemary Hill on the east. For the western boundary an agreement had to be reached with the Castle which was being built or about to be built at the same time. The Priory boundary followed the way from 'The Queen and Castle' corner along the old track down to the Ford, but instead of following the old track across the low ground to the 'Borrow Well', it was kept to the right, southwards up to a ridge then turned sharp east, crossing the brook further south to join the old road at the 'Borrow Well'. Thus the Priory area covered a large piece of low lying ground, depriving the villages of yet another ancient right of way. The new direction of road meant that the drovers had to drive their cattle up hill and down again, instead of on the level.

The Augustinian monks wanted flat, dry, level ground near a stream on which to build their priory. Abbeys like Fountains Abbey, Bolton Abbey and Tintern Abbey were all built in such locations. The area best suited in 'Chinewrda' was where the village lay along the east-west track on the north bank of Finham Brook. This area now belonged to them and there they built their priory, across the track and village, depriving the villagers of a further ancient way. The detour was along the northern boundary of their newly acquired property, now High Street and Castle Hill.

The enclosing of the area taken by the Priory closed off three ways to the public. But it seems that two ways, one from the War Memorial to Townpool Bridge and part of the old Roman way along the north bank of Finham Brook were used by the monks, as they still exist.

The best place for the Priory to have a water-mill was precisely where they built it. The eastern end of the Abbey Pool finished at naturally higher ground than the pool and where the brook broke through they built their water mill. To the west of this point the land was marshy, to the east it was flat and drier.

According to the late Helmut Mykura, in **Kenilworth History 1992**, the brook between the Ford and the Mill was diverted to form a mill leat. Certainly the evidence there bears this out.

The brook acted as a barrier between the Priory buildings on the north side and the meadows to the south side, the mill forming a crossing point over the brook. Access to the mill would naturally have been from the top of what is now called Abbey End. From the north, access would have been down from High Street in line with the east bank of the Pool.

The south transept, the cloisters and the courtyard of the Priory were built over the old Roman track. The track was widened to form the courtyard with the Gatehouse built on the north side and the 'Barn' on the south side. The roadway up from the mill formed the west edge of the courtyard.

During the life of the Priory the Roman track to the west of the courtyard for a limited distance, possibly as far as the small stream down from Bull Hill, must have been made use of. It is along the top of the bank in this direction that the very old trees, perhaps planted as saplings by the monks in the sixteenth century, still grow above the marsh level. Off the south side of this track, just to the west of the north-south roadway, was built a boathouse beside the pool. The old Roman track to the east of the Priory buildings probably was also used. It would appear that after the Dissolution in 1538, during the plundering of the stonework, the two parts of the track were once again united.

In the early part of the twentieth century a row of trees was planted each side of part of this reinstated trackway, through the courtyard and where the cloisters were built. The packhorse bridge by the mill was demolished in a flood in 1673.

7. THE CASTLE c.1124

The Normans picked an ideal place to build a castle; a high promontory projecting out into the valley of a stream, with marshy land to the east and west and in the south a narrow marshy valley about 200 metres (650ft) wide, through which the Finham Brook runs.

Later by building a dam, in the early thirteenth century, across this point of the valley a great area of land upstream was flooded, forming the Mere. Defence mounds and ditches were built along the natural contours to the best advantage, with a water-mill included.

The building of the dam must have caused some consternation, as the rising water cut off the trackway to Honiley at the bottom of Purlieu Lane. 300 years later it was reinstated with a bridge built by the Earl of Leicester, but whether the villagers were allowed access is another matter. The obvious alternative route would have been the ancient "Track K" from St. John's Well to the Finham Brook bridge in Chase Lane, but that had been obliterated during the previous thousand years.

The hamlet of Blackwell may have drawn travellers from the Honiley direction, using part of "Track K" to the crossing of the stream just past St. John's Well, which still exists in some form, and continuing north-east towards Blackwell where Chase Lane would be met. Then along the 'newly' formed track of Chase Lane into Kenilworth. Alternatively, perhaps, they used the 'Mesolithic' track from the Honiley direction to the Warwick Road, that is now Rouncil Lane. This track was probably also a sensible boundary for the Castle Park.

8. CRYFIELD POOL

The pool belonging to the Hermits of Cryfield was part in the parish of Kenilworth and part in the parish of Stoneleigh. The Hermits probably used a section of the old way to Canley along "Track C" to collect fish from their pool (SP29557364). However, this track seems to have gone out of use in the Stoneleigh Parish in the late twelfth century but remained in the Kenilworth Parish in the form of the lower end of Crackley Lane to the present day.

Another more convenient track was made between the Hermitage and the Pool. This way may still exist, as at certain points along the present track there are dressed stones. The demise of "Track C" may have been due to two factors. More travelling was taking place between Kenilworth and Coventry along English Lane and less between Kenilworth and Canley along "Track C". Also in 1130 the Priory of Kenilworth acquired a Hermitage at Fletchamsted.

The route to Fletchamsted could have been along the remaining section of "Track C", that is the southern end of Crackley Lane, and the existing footpath from Crackley Farm northwards, keeping east of the present woods of Crackley and Roughknowles. On this route, over a small stream at (SP29157440) are the remains of a stone bridge.

In the **Stoneleigh Leger Book** and the **Victoria History of the County of Warwick**, Volume 2, it is stated that in the reign of Stephen a piece of land called Radmore, in Cannock Chase, was granted to two hermits Clement and Hervey and their companions, together with a piece of land called Mellesho for tillage and pasturing their cattle. However, the hermits soon found their devotions were disturbed by the foresters of the Chase. They besought the Empress Matilda to change their site, but they stayed there for twelve years and during that time an abbey was founded. On 19 December 1154, the day of his accession, they petitioned Henry II to transfer them to his Manor of Stoneleigh in Warwickshire. Their wish was granted and after first trying Cryfield, which was too close to a highway, the monks settled at a place near the confluence of the Rivers Avon and Sowe, where they built an abbey. The Hermitage became a Grange of Stoneleigh Abbey. Access was needed between Abbey and Grange, but regular journeying through the territory of the Augustinian Priory of Kenilworth was probably not desired, therefore a short way of skirting the Kenilworth parish was sought. A look at a large scale O.S. map 1/25,000 will show a possible route direct from Cryfield Grange to Westley Bridge by following Cryfield Grange Road on the west of the present railway line and a line of hedgerow to the east of the railway line to the bridge then on to Stoneleigh. This line from Cryfield Grange along the hedgeline to Westley Bridge aligns with the bridge at Stoneleigh village over the River Sowe, suggesting it is an ancient trackway. The junction of this track with

"Track C" may be the reason for selecting this site for a hermitage in the first place, but again it was found to be too noisy. It is at the crossing of this track with "Track K" that the Neolithic axe head was found.

All evidence of the Pool disappeared when the embankment for the railway line from Kenilworth junction to Berkswell, opened in 1884, was built across it.

9. NEW STREET

It appears from the available information, and from the conclusions arrived at from the evidence shown by the ground, the original 'NEW STREET' was the old 'Roman Way'. That is, from where the 'Roman Way' crossed the 'Prehistoric Way' 'Line C' and roughly along where Pears Close now lies. So as not to confuse ourselves let us call this original piece of 'Roman Way' 'R Street'.

It is possible that the route used for travelling from the village of 'Chinewrda' to Canley was along 'R Street' to join the Prehistoric Way 'Line C', and then following it northwards. This route, it seems, may have been used in Saxon times and continued to be used until the mid-twelfth century when the Washbrook crossing probably came into being to serve the Adibarne area. From the Enclosure Award of 1756 this crossing is referred to as 'HARPERSFORD'.

Crossing from the south bank of Finham Brook over to the north bank at Washbrook would bring travellers on to the old Roman North Bank track. Turning west would bring them on to track 'Line C' to journey to Canley. It seems natural that in time, a short cut was worn to the track 'Line C', a short cut we now call 'Tainters Hill'. Probably also about this time a trackway was forming from the bottom of Tainters Hill along a very short length of 'R Street', around the foot of the hill (Strawberry Bank) and then bearing northwards by-passing the village to the east to eventually meet 'Via Regia de Kenilworth' to Allesley. The southern end of this track became 'Manor Road' and the northern part 'Love Lane'.

In *c*.1124 the Priory was being built across the old Roman track. A new 'road' was made higher up the hillside now High Street. Eastwards from the road up from the Abbey Gate House was called 'Alta Strata', meaning 'High Level', and 'Brodegate' westwards from the same point. This meant that travelling eastwards from 'Alta Strata' one had to turn south near the site of the traffic lights towards the Brook to pick up 'R Street'. This, of course, was inconvenient. A 'New Way' was eventually made, possibly later that century or early thirteenth century, from the traffic lights site to meet the old Roman Way near the bottom of Tainters Hill.

The first 60 metres of the present New Street, from the traffic lights, follow this line. In the first instance this diversion would be referred to as the 'New Way' as opposed to the lower route. To quote from John Drew's book **Yesterday's Town** *". . . It could have got the name 'New Way' according to Mr. Butler . . . as the road previously ran behind the old cottages"* (but at what date did Mr. Butler say this?)

House building perhaps then began on this 'New Way' and became known as 'Newestrete'. In **A Kenilworth Chronology** Harry Sunley's entry for 1383 includes *"It is testified at the Assize that John Carpenter of Newestrete threatened to kill John Oacres . . ."*

Up to the fourteenth century the Odiborne area had been all woods and the only 'road' through it would have been 'Track C', the present south part of Crackley Lane. There must have been pathways, however, dividing up the coppices. The Abbey turned the area into a rabbit warren, and by 1539 the woods had been cleared. In a survey of 1592 there is mention of a *'Tyle Howse'* in Odybarne held by Edward Sheppard who also had the right to take clay to make tiles. In the 1756 Enclosure Awards it gives ". . . *on the common called Tainters Hill Common . . . and the 'Tilekiln House' in the occupation of Daniel Arnold'*. This is rather strange, as this area is mainly sand. There is a house built partly of stone and partly of timber still in existence, 'Spring Cottage', at the north end of Love Lane where it joined at right angles a short lane west into Via Regia Kenilworth. On the 'Fish map' of 1692 this short lane is called ODIBURNE LANE. Upper Spring Lane did not exist until about 1800. Wm. Yates' map of 1793 shows a short length of road from Fieldgate Lane to Spring Cottage, but no further. However 41 years later, the plan showing the proposed modification to the Turnpike Road through this area of Kenilworth dated 24th November 1834, (a modification which never took place) shows Upper Spring Lane existing as it does today.

On the six inch O.S. map of 1930 there is a well indicated (SP 28857284) by the hedge to the Coventry Road in what is known as 'Parliament Piece' which suggests a dwelling once stood there. On William Yates' map of 1793 and on John Cary's map of 1811 a building is shown in this vicinity by the side of the road, indicating that there must have been some fairly important activity going on in this area. Was this, then, the attraction that caused, in about the seventeenth century, the curving northwards of the east end of New Street where it met Manor Road and Love Lane, on the west side of 'Strawberry Bank' and perhaps to continue as a foot path to where the top of Tainters Hill met the ancient Prehistoric 'Line C' passing this building with its well en route? It was from this junction with Manor Road and Love Lane and the once again diverted New Street that the new road to the Kenilworth-Stoneleigh boundary was cut sometime between the years 1761 and 1793.

'The Old Manor House' (up until the 1930s known as 'Vine Cottage) in Manor Road lies just east of the Prehistoric 'Line C' on the corner where it crosses Manor Road. The original part of this building is very old; were there still traces of 'Track C' when it was built?

10. ENGLISH LANE
AND THE TURNPIKE ROAD

Part of the present Kenilworth Road, inside the boundary of Stoneleigh, goes north-east for about half a kilometre after leaving the line of "Track K" 200m (200 yards) from Crackley Bridge before turning more northerly. This 'half kilometre' part heads for and runs along the Coventry-Stoneleigh boundary near the Green Lane area of Coventry. I suggest it is the line of a Roman Way. My reason for this is that it is straight and does not fit the usual criteria to be a Prehistoric Trackway.

It partially existed up to the late eighteenth century, or early nineteenth century. Cary's map of 1811 does not show it. However the William Yates' map of 1793 marks the position and labels it 'ENGLISH LANE', and shows the new Turnpike Road to Coventry. The earlier maps, that of Thomas Kitchin of 1760 and perhaps that of Thomas Jefferys of 1752 suggest that the present Kenilworth Road from Crackley Bridge to Coventry existed then.

It is said, quote, *"New Street, earlier known as New Way, was cut as a Turnpike in 1727"*. There is confusion here, as there is evidence of three 'New Ways' in this area. All could have been called the 'New Way' when first cut, ranging over the 600 years from *c*.1130 to *c*.1730.

New Street in Kenilworth was a 'New Way' in the first instance. (*See* chapter on New Street). This Turnpike Road from Crackley to Coventry was a 'New Way' when first cut in 1727. The third 'New Way' is dealt with later in this chapter.

During the thirteenth century the part of the town south of Abbey Fields was becoming the more important. The journey from Castle End to Coventry was down Rosemary Hill along School Lane and The Close following Finham Brook to the ford at Mill End, then up through the Common over Crackley Bridge (Gatebridge) and English Lane to Stivichall. It appears it remained this way up to 1727 when the route was improved by the building of a 'New Way', the Turnpike Road from Coventry to Crackley Bridge, at that time called Milburn Bridge and before that 'Gatebridge' as can be seen on the Thomas Jefferys' map of 1752. English Lane then became redundant.

Thomas Jefferys' 1752 map also shows that Kenilworth, too, had made improvements to this route. 'Albion Row' changed to 'Albion Street' in 1917, had been cut through and superseded School Lane. This cut out having to go down the steep Rosemary Hill and swinging precariously right into School Lane ('Pepper Alley' at the time, and 'Stockyngende' in the sixteenth century) in a 'four-in-hand', or the drag up in the reverse direction at the end of a journey from Coventry. The ford at Mill End and the Common had still to be negotiated. A rather hazardous journey.

The direct way to Warwick from Coventry would have been through Finham, Stoneleigh, Ashow, etc., along the north-west bank of the River Avon. In 1250 the Constable of the Castle ordered that the heavily wooded area alongside the Coventry to Warwick road be cut back for the safe passage of travellers. Was it along this road that the cutting back of trees was to take place? Apart from the Common there was no heavily wooded area in the parish of Kenilworth en route.

Returning to the journey from Coventry to Kenilworth, something obviously had to be done about the route through the Common and the Mill End ford. The 1793 William Yates' map shows that alterations had been made, possibly by 1756. Another 'New Way' had been cut from the junction of Love Lane with Manor Road to the Kenilworth-Stoneleigh boundary, meeting the Roman Way on the curve up to the Common, thereby giving a 'good' road from New Street to the boundary and on to Coventry.

The way through the Common was now by-passed and reverted to a track again, probably only used by those living in the Mill End area. The journey from Coventry to Castle End Kenilworth was now made on a 'good road' all the way. This route meant reverting to climbing and descending Rosemary Hill again, dangerous for a horse-drawn vehicle, but evidence at the hill top indicates that at some time it was 'eased', judging by the footpath on the eastern side. No doubt the coaches would draw in at the 'Bowling Green Inn' for a refresher after the pull up the hill.

The old way to the Common and the ford at Mill End from Crackley Bridge was abandoned in favour of the new main road. Instead a roadway, now known as Common Lane, was cut from this new main road higher up the hill heading for the junction of Knowle Hill and Dalehouse Lane. But it stopped at the meeting point with the old road through the Common. This was required to serve the people of Mill End.

The railway construction map of 1841 shows the first part of Common Lane as a good road up to the meeting with the old way. After that it follows a route, as it does today but only as a foot track down to Dalehouse Lane. To have gone straight, as it appears was originally intended, would have meant a very steep hill. The footpath must have been a secondary consideration, for when the second railway bridge was built, with only future horse and foot traffic in mind, the bad alignment between the two bridges did not matter, and the second bridge, like the first, was built to suit the railway track underneath.

The building of the railway between 1841 and 1844 finally obliterated English Lane.

11. VIA REGIA

The Norman Royal Ways or King's Highways, it is said, had to be wide enough to allow sixteen knights in full armour to ride abreast. Allowing just four feet wide (1.2m) for each horseman a road at least sixty four feet wide (19.2m) would be required.

Hollis Lane which is supposed to have been part of 'VIA REGIA de KENELWORTH', the Kings Highway, is only '3 rods' that is fifty feet between hedges. Taking away the ditches either side, which would have been there, leaves only forty feet (12.2m) at the most. Further north in the heathland they may have been able to spread out. This seems to suggest that the main highways may have been wide, but there were sections where the width was much reduced.

Where would the king and his entourage be making for, north of Kenilworth? There were Norman castles at Maxstoke, Fillongley and Astley to the north, Baginton, Brandon and Brinklow to the east and north-east, and Clopton, Beaudesert and Studley to the west. Out of all these it would seem the first three would be the most likely destinations. Each of these would be a journey of ten to twelve miles (16-19km) from Kenilworth Castle, and roughly the distance between overnight stops for such a cavalcade.

Which route north out of Kenilworth, then, would be the King's Highway? These days the best way to Maxstoke from Kenilworth Castle would be along Clinton Lane, Red Lane, Hodgetts Lane to Berkswell, Meriden and Maxstoke. To get to Fillongley and Astley follow the same route as above to Meriden, then turn off to Fillongley and a few miles further on to Astley; or Hollis Lane to Westwood Heath and winding one's way to Allesley through country lanes to Corley then to Fillongley or Astley.

Looking at a possible route in early Norman times, using tracks that could have been in existence at the time, seems to be the best method of approaching this problem of ascertaining the King's Highway to the north. Considering each section in turn, we can then eliminate or confirm.

My suggestion for Fillongley and Astley is, along Hollis Lane to Dunn's pits, then straight across to the south-east corner of Broadwells Wood, along the western edge of the woods, carrying on northwards to a pond just south of Bockendon Grange Farm, then directly across to Bockendon Lane crossing Westwood Heath Road towards Allesley through heathland, where the tracks are now obliterated.

Hollis Lane up as far as Dunn's Pits is, as mentioned before, about forty feet (12.2m) between ditches. These ditches may have been dug by the Saxons or the Normans to drain the King's Highway. They appear again around the south and west side of Broadwells Wood. A lane here in the 1785 Perambulation is referred to as BROADWELLS LANE. The stretch of road between Dunn's Pits and Broadwells Wood has now been ploughed up, although east of the railway track the hedge line still exists. In the 1785 Perambulations it is called HAY LANE. On the 1891 O.S. map it is still marked but with the railway, which was opened in 1884, cutting through it, the present continuation of Hollis Lane into Crackley Lane now takes all the traffic. There is mentioned *a Slough called St. Anne's Hole* through which a member of the perambulation party waded. In the length of Hay Lane from the old railway track to Dunn's Pits there is a deep depression in the ground, on the line of a stream, at the lowest point of which are still the remains of an Australian type wind pump. Could this be St. Anne's Hole?

The east hedge and a length of ditch of the road can be followed from the south-east corner of Broadwells Wood around the west side, and north to the farm gate just short of the pond. The gate crosses where the road may have been, because the hedgeline now continues on the west side of our 'road' for a short distance up to the pond. Taking a line from the pond directly across the field to Bockendon Lane brings one to a hedge alongside a small stream which is bridged by a public footbridge into the apparent twenty foot wide (6m) road through the old hamlet of Bockendon, lining up absolutely with Bockendon Lane.

On the 1793 Yates map a dog-leg is shown off this track 220yds (200m) north of the stream through Broadwells Wood. It turns off north-east and follows a hedgeline for 110yds (100m) before turning north through the hedge to meet the track again at the footbridge at Bockendon Farm. As a thoroughfare it must have existed up to c.1891, as it is shown on the O.S. map of that date, in fact there are two large old trees marking the route. I have not found any early map showing the road from Broadwells Wood up to the pond and across to Bockendon Lane, but evidence is there to show it once must have existed along the line of the present footpath. Then at some time prior to 1793, the road past the pond was diverted for some reason to the dog-leg.

Early one November morning in 1992 while walking towards this pond along the footpath by the divergence, the low early morning sun showed up a raised bank in the meadow to the west of and parallel to the footpath. I judged it to be about 35ft (11m) distant from me. At first I thought it was a causeway linking ridge and furrow farming, but I noticed also that it was in line with the footpath crossing the old railway track and the 'windmill' hill to the south and the pond behind me. Further investigation showed it also aligned the hill on which the War Memorial stands. It appears that not only was it the west hedge bank of the road but the line of a trackway very much older than Norman or Saxon or even Roman times, and the pond was a 'sighting pond'. Since this observation it has now been almost ploughed out.

The earliest reliable map, the James Fish map of 1692, shows Hollis Lane up to a little short of Dunn's Pits, but apparently continuing on north. At this particular point it is joined by a footpath from the west. In the north of the map the west side of Broadwells Wood is shown, but instead of showing the road around the south side, it shows a footpath going south passing Dunn's Pits Farm on its east and keeping a small hill on its west before turning east on to Hollis Lane. This hill was known as Windmill Hill. It seems highly likely that travellers walking from the Bockendon area would follow the road from the pond down to the bottom west corner of Broadwells Wood, and then make straight for the windmill on Windmill Hill, after which they would bear left into Hollis Lane, while horse and wheeled traffic still used the 'main road'. '*Wyndmyllfeld, 60 acres*' is referred to in a document of 22nd July 1549 listing property acquired by Andrew Flammok. It would seem likely, then, the footpath existed at least from this date, and could be the remnants of the old track mentioned earlier. This footpath does not turn up again until the 1893 O.S. map.

So far there is nothing to discount any of the Broadwells Lane route, but we must bear in mind that in early Norman times a vast part of this area was heathland.

A look at a present-day map shows a track from the north end of Hay Lane continuing into Broadwells Wood, this may also have been part of Hay Lane. It is doubtful if this was the way north as it would lead into bad ground around the confluence of two streams in the centre of the wood.

Although Bockendon Lane is just outside the area under consideration, it must be included as it is involved with the old roads out of the north of Kenilworth.

Bockendon Lane, from Westwood Heath road southwards to Broadwells Wood and northwards into the Westwood Heath, must have been an important roadway. Also Crackley Lane, as it is fairly wide all the way from Crackley Woods up to Bockendon Lane as there is evidence here that there was a cross roads at this point. A field gate in the hedge directly in line with Crackley Lane indicates that there could have been a way through. A hedge and ditch on the south side of this continuation leads up to Black Waste Wood and joins the still visible hollow way on the south-east edge of the wood. A public footpath follows this line, albeit on the other side of the hedge. On the east side of Crackley Lane near the railway bridge the vestige of a hollow way, or hedge and ditches can still be seen just inside the woods.

The track on the north side of Westwood Heath Road has now been lost, although a cart track is indicated in this position, leading to Park Wood, on a 1959 O.S. map. From Westwood Heath Road the Bockendon Lane route can be walked down to the south-west corner of Broadwells Wood as it is now a public footpath. From this point the footpath follows the direct line to the 'windmill', crossing the stiles and old railway track. But here the direction now changes. Up to about 1972 the old way directly to the 'windmill' existed as 'Footpath K7', the hedges at this time were being grubbed up and K7 was diverted to its present way.

Red Lane in the twelfth century was called RED LANE only from Burton Green down to 'RED LANE ENDE', a point where the Kenilworth boundary following Red Lane down from Burton Green turns sharp east. From there along the old route to RUDFIN LANE (now the Birmingham Road) between the twelfth and seventeenth centuries was called FIRSENFEYLD LANE or variations of it. The bottom corner of it was called 'Mare Meadow Corner'. In the twelfth and thirteenth centuries it was 'the way to Prestwell'. (Was there a priest's well that way?)

In 1581, this southern length is shown as no more than a footpath. The 1628 'Harding' map shows this lower section as being less important than Hollis Lane, the top section from Burton Green down to Red Lane End being more important. From Red Lane End a route is shown zig-zagging south-east to Dunn's Pits, picking up Hollis Lane into Kenilworth.

The journey to Maxstoke was probably made by heading for Berkswell but not via Red Lane as we might do now, for as mentioned before, Firsenfeyld Lane was only a footpath in those days. Instead they would have made their way up Hollis Lane to Dunn's Pits and zig-zagged up FOSSATA, as this length was called, to Burton Green and along Hodgetts Lane to Berkswell. But did they?

There is evidence of a straight trackway, probably little more than a footpath in its latter days, from the south-west corner of Broadwells Wood across to the sharp right-hand bend 750yds (700m) down from the top of Red Lane. It passes through a large gap in the hedge on the east side of the railway and the railway itself took the trouble to bridge it! At the end by the wood there is the remains of a 'hunting gate' leading onto it out of the old Broadwells Lane.

On the 1834 O.S. map is shown a short spur off in this direction at this point. In fact a careful look at the 1628 Harding map shows another short spur branching off to the east 750yds (700m) down Red Lane. Was this part of Via Regia to Maxstoke in Norman times? Was this the Fossata and not the route mentioned earlier? Contour-wise this last suggestion is as plausible and probable as the possible route of Fossata, which follows the zig-zag of the field boundaries across to Hollis Lane. There is no certainty about it, but it is more direct. That is a suggestion I put forward.

The situation is complicated by the fact that in one account in 1785 part of Hay Lane (called HURST LANE in 1581) is referred to as part of the Fossata in early Norman times. While the lane along the south of Crackley Woods, now part of Crackley Lane, is called HOLYES LANE in c.1581 (Hollis Lane?); but then this same lane is named as MANNY PENNY MELLE in the twelfth-fourteenth centuries! It is quite a different lane from the present day Hollis Lane.

There is another VIA REGIA nearby. The southern end of Crackley Lane is part of the ancient "Track C" to Canley. It was along this highway that the noisy travellers disturbed the Hermits of Cryfield causing them to petition the King yet again to move them, this time to Etchills Wood. (*See* Chapter 7 'Cryfield Pool'). This highway, incidentally, looks the more likely 'Via Regia' to those castles in the north, say Fillongley and Astley, than that along Hollis Lane.

There is yet another highway, VIA ALTA SIVE REGIA, now Dalehouse Lane. This would take the cavalcade to the Baginton, Brandon and Brinklow direction. Starting from the Castle in Kenilworth, a probable route would be eastwards along the new 'Brodegate' and Alta Strata' to ford Finham Brook at Washbrook or to the ford at Mill End. Along Via Alta Sive Regia to Finham Bridge which is on the prehistoric way along the north-west bank of the River Avon, crossing Finham Brook once again to go north. Via Alta Sive Regia went all the way to Finham Bridge up to the late eighteenth century when the section from Westley Bridge to Finham Bridge became a footpath, and the Stoneleigh Road took a new course from Westley Bridge to Gibbet Hill, abandoning the prehistoric way to Cryfield Hermitage.

If "Track K" had been in existence from about where it crosses "Track C" eastwards in the eleventh century, I believe this would have been used, and would still be in use today.

Looking east. The "Roman Way" followed the line of trees on top of the bank on the left towards the 'Barn' and 'Gatehouse'.

12. OTHER ROADS

Beehive Hill and Malthouse Lane may have been, if they existed, no more than footpaths up until they were made shortly after 1756.

In the Enclosure Award of 1756 there is a reference '. . . *by the New Intended Road to lead from BULL HILL to the New intended road leading from ODIBORNE LANE to RUDFIN LANE'*.

The 'New Intended Road leading from Odiborne Lane to Rudfin Lane' is, of course, Beehive Hill, and the New Intended Road leading from Bull Hill to the 'New Intended Road . . .' is Malthouse Lane.

In 1692, according to the 'Fish' map of that date, Firsenfeyld Lane still followed the east side of the small stream and up past the old, and still existing, 'Long Meadow Barn' joining Red Lane at Red Lane End.

The construction of the new route of Red Lane from Red Lane End to the bottom end, and being called Red Lane from Burton Green all the way down to the Birmingham Road, appears to have taken place about the same time as the construction of Beehive Hill and Malthouse Lane, that is shortly after 1756.

The line of the old 'Firsenfeyld Lane' can still be traced at the bottom of Red Lane on the east side of the Birmingham Road.

Thomas Kitchin shows Red Lane on his 1760 map, but it is difficult to judge whether it is the old 'Firsenfeyld Lane' or the new Red Lane. However, William Yates definitely shows the new road on his 1793 map.

Time will eliminate further tangible evidence, but in time more written evidence, no doubt, will emerge to disprove, or back up or confirm my theories.

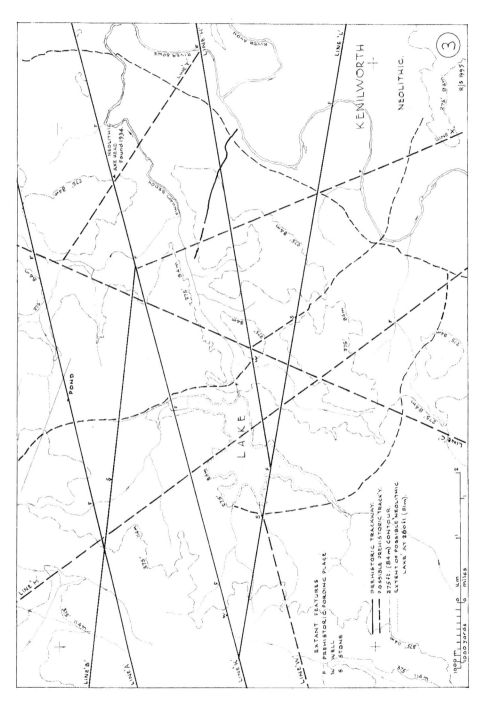

EXTANT FEATURES
F - PREHISTORIC FORDING PLACE
W WELL
S STONE

———— PREHISTORIC TRACKWAY.
– – – POSSIBLE PREHISTORIC TRACKY.
275ft. (84m) CONTOUR.
·········· EXTENT OF POSSIBLE NEOLITHIC
LAKE AT 260ft (81m).

KENILWORTH

NEOLITHIC.

RJS 1995

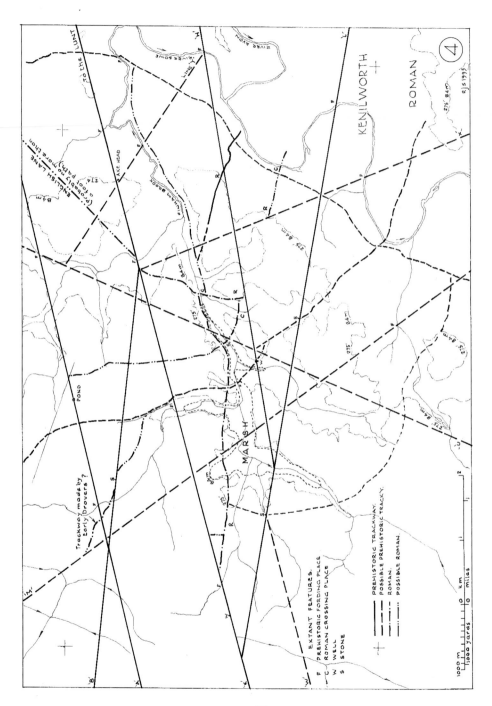

KENILWORTH

ROMAN

RIVER AVON

RIVER SOWE

to the LUNT

ENGLISH LANE (probably no more than a foot path?)

LAKE HEAD

POND

Trackway made by Early Drovers?

MARSH

EXTANT FEATURES.
F   PREHISTORIC FORDING PLACE
C   ROMAN CROSSING PLACE
W   WELL
S   STONE

―――― PREHISTORIC TRACKWAY.
― ― ― POSSIBLE PREHISTORIC TRACKWAY.
―·―·― ROMAN.
―··―··― POSSIBLE ROMAN.

1000 m
0
1000 yards
0
km
miles

R.S.1993.

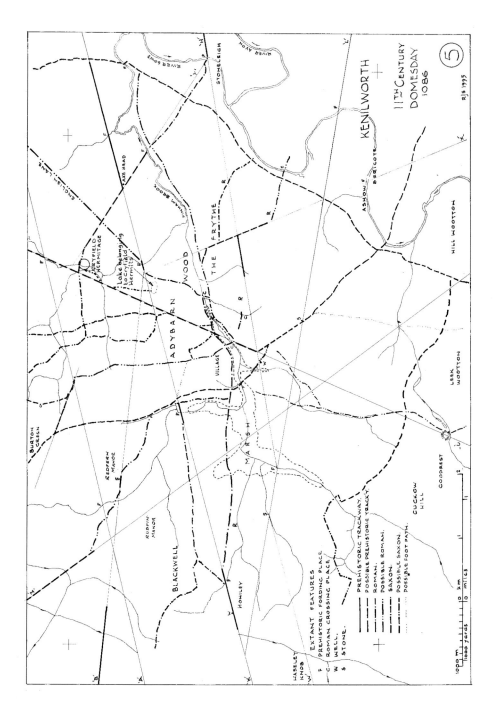

11TH CENTURY
DOMESDAY
1086

KENILWORTH

EXTANT FEATURES
F PREHISTORIC FORDING PLACE
C ROMAN CROSSING PLACE
W WELL.
S STONE.

————— PREHISTORIC TRACKWAY.
– – – – POSSIBLE PREHISTORIC TRACK.
—·—·— ROMAN.
······· POSSIBLE ROMAN.
—··—··— SAXON.
·········· POSSIBLE SAXON.
······· POSSIBLE FOOT PATH.

1000 M
1000 YARDS
0 km
0 miles

R|S 1995

RIVER SOWE
STONELEIGH
RIVER AVON
ASHOW
BERICOTE
HILL WOOTTON
LEEK WOOTTON
GOODREST
CUCKOW HILL
HOMILEY
HASELEY KNOB
BLACKWELL
RUDFIN MANOR
REDFERN MANOR
BURTON GREEN
ENGLISH LANE
CRYFIELD HERMITAGE
Lake belonging to Cryfield Hermits
AXE HEAD
LITTLE BROOK
ADYBARN WOOD
THE FRYTHE
MARSH
VILLAGE

39

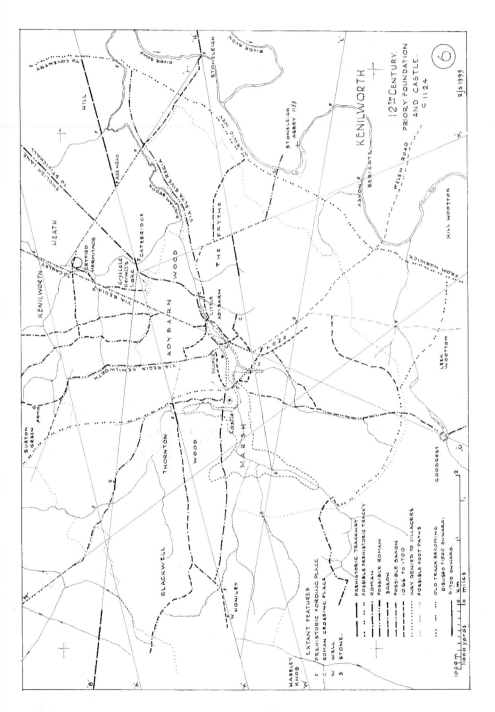

KENILWORTH

12TH CENTURY.
PRIORY FOUNDATION
AND CASTLE.
C.1124

R/s 1995

EXTANT FEATURES
F PREHISTORIC FORDING PLACE
C ROMAN CROSSING PLACE
W WELL
S STONE.

· · · · · PREHISTORIC TRACKWAY
· · · · · POSSIBLE PREHISTORIC TRACKY
- · - · - ROMAN
- · - · - POSSIBLE ROMAN
- - - - - SAXON
- · · - · · POSSIBLE SAXON
· · · · · 1066 TO 1700
· · · · · WAY DENIED TO VILLAGERS.
· · · · · POSSIBLE FOOT PATHS
· · · · · OLD TRACK BECOMING
         DISUSED C.1500 ONWARD.
         C.1700 ONWARD.

1000 m
1000 yards
1 km   1 mile
HASELEY
KNOB

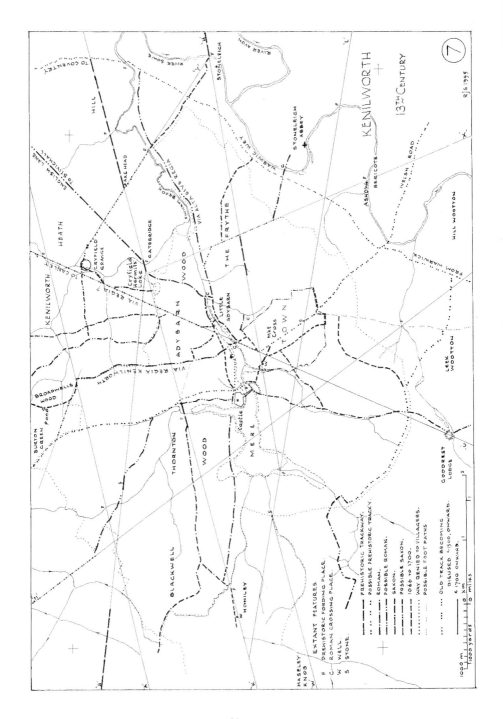

KENILWORTH
13TH CENTURY

RJS 1995

7

EXTANT FEATURES
F PREHISTORIC FORDING PLACE.
C ROMAN CROSSING PLACE.
W WELL.
S STONE.

· · · · · · ·   PREHISTORIC TRACKWAY.
· · · · · · ·   POSSIBLE PREHISTORIC TRACKY.
—·—·—·—·—·   ROMAN.
—·—·—·—·—·   POSSIBLE ROMAN.
—————   SAXON.
—·—·—·—·—·   POSSIBLE SAXON.
—————   1066 TO 1700.
· · · · · · ·   WAY DENIED TO VILLAGERS.
· · · · · · ·   POSSIBLE FOOT PATHS.

· · · · · ·   OLD TRACK BECOMING
              DISUSED C.1500. ONWARD.
—————   C. 1700 ONWARD.

1000 m   0 km   2
1000 yards   0 miles   1

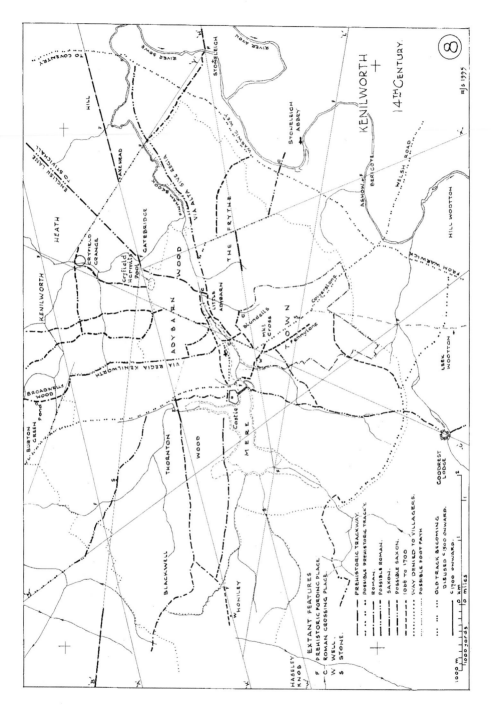

KENILWORTH
14TH CENTURY

⑧

RJS 1995

EXTANT FEATURES
F PREHISTORIC FORDING PLACE.
C ROMAN CROSSING PLACE.
W WELL.
S STONE.

... ... PREHISTORIC TRACKWAY.
... ... POSSIBLE PREHISTORIC TRACKY.
... ... ROMAN.
... ... POSSIBLE ROMAN.
... ... SAXON.
... ... POSSIBLE SAXON.
... ... 1066 TO 1700.
... ... WAY DENIED TO VILLAGERS,
           1066 to 1700.
... ... POSSIBLE FOOT PATH.

... ... OLD TRACK BECOMING
           DISUSED c.1500 ONWARD.
           c.1700 ONWARD.

1000 m
0   km   2
1000 yards
0   miles   1

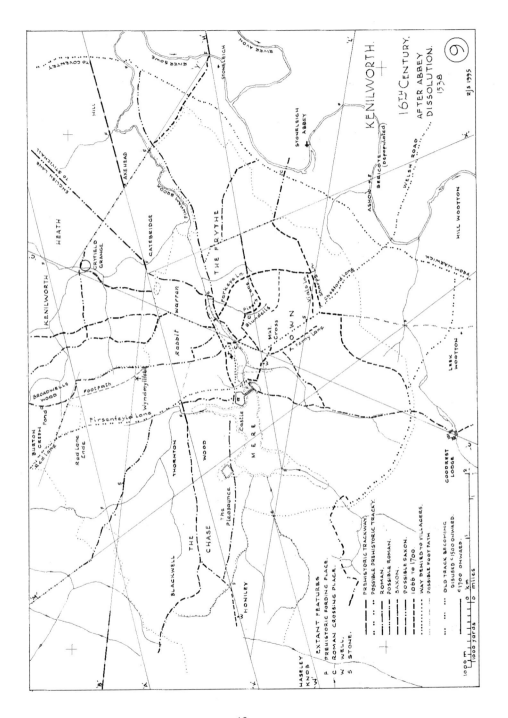

KENILWORTH.

16TH CENTURY.

AFTER ABBEY
DISSOLUTION.
1538

RJS 1995

⑥

EXTANT FEATURES.
F PREHISTORIC FORDING PLACE.
C ROMAN CROSSING PLACE.
W WELL.
S STONE.

· — · — · PREHISTORIC TRACKWAY.
· · — · · POSSIBLE PREHISTORIC TRACKWAY.
— — — — ROMAN.
— — — — POSSIBLE ROMAN.
——————— SAXON.
· · · · · · POSSIBLE SAXON.
————— 1066 TO 1700.
· · · · · · · WAY DENIED TO VILLAGERS.
· · · · · · · POSSIBLE FOOT PATH.
· · · ··· OLD TRACK BECOMING
           DISUSED c.1500 ONWARD.
           c.1700 ONWARD.

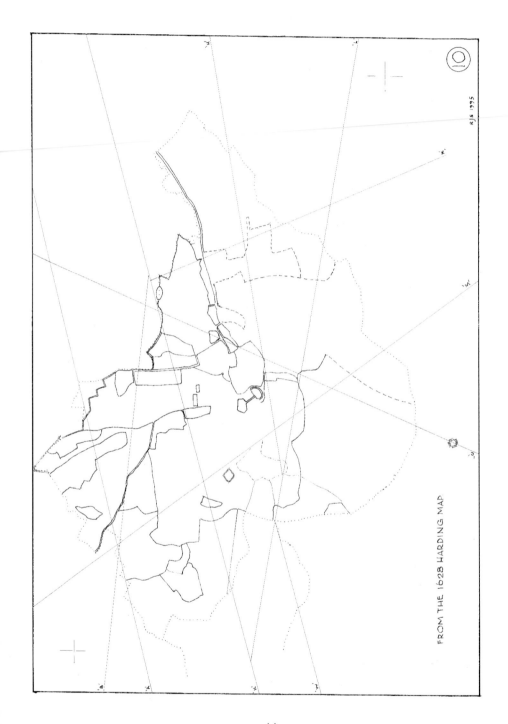

FROM THE 1628 HARDING MAP

RJS 1995

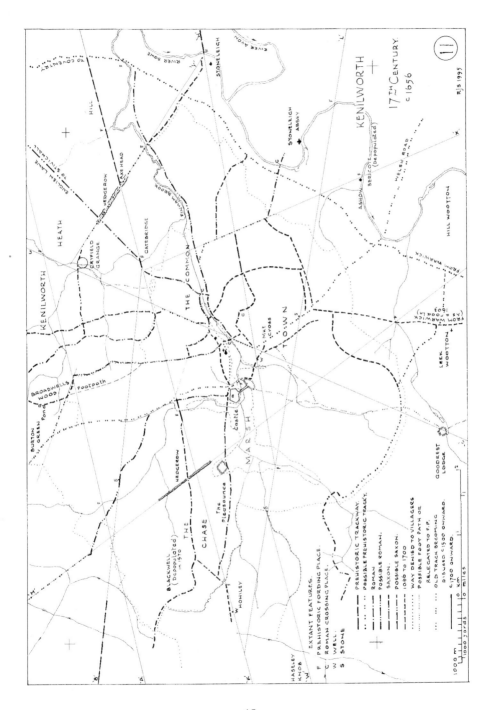

KENILWORTH

17TH CENTURY
c 1656

RJS 1995

TO COVENTRY
BUDBROOK LANE TO STIVICHALL
HILL
HEATH
KENILWORTH
BROADWELLS WOOD
Footpath
BURTON GREEN
Burton Pond
BLACKWELL (Depopulated in 1670)
THE CHASE
HEDGEROW
The Playhouse
HOHLEY
HASELEY KNOB

HEDGEROW
LAKE HEAD
CATESBRIDGE
CRYFIELD GRANGE
FINHAM BROOK
THE COMMON
MARSH
Castle

STONELEIGH
RIVER SOWE
RIVER AVON
STONELEIGH ABBEY

TOWN
Mkt Cross

ASHOW
BERICOTE (Depopulated)
WELSH ROAD
KENILWORTH
HILL WOOTTON
FROM WARWICK
LEEK WOOTTON
(ASHWOOD 1609)
GOODREST LODGE
FROM WARWICK

EXTANT FEATURES.
F PREHISTORIC FORDING PLACE.
C ROMAN CROSSING PLACE.
W WELL.
S STONE.

— — — PREHISTORIC TRACKWAY.
— · — POSSIBLE PREHISTORIC TRACK.
— — — ROMAN.
— · — POSSIBLE ROMAN.
— — — SAXON.
········ POSSIBLE SAXON.
— — — 1086 TO 1700
········ WAY DENIED TO VILLAGERS
········ POSSIBLE FOOT PATH OR
          RELEGATED TO F.P.
— · · — OLD TRACK BECOMING
          DISUSED C1500 ONWARD.
— — — C.1700 ONWARD.

1000 m
1000 yards
0 miles
0 km

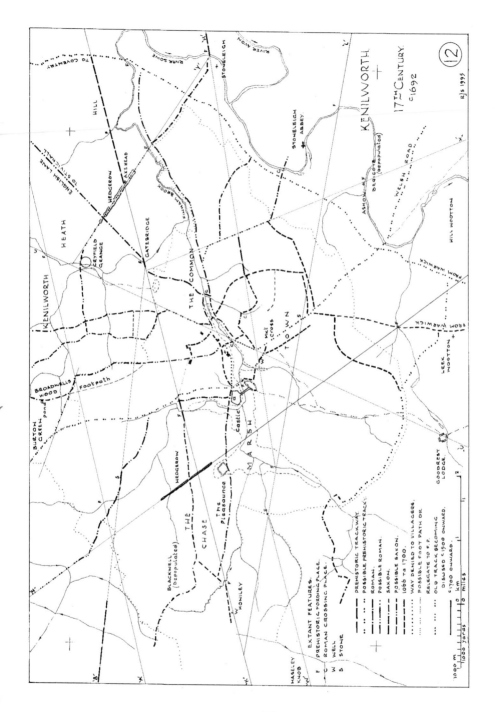

KENILWORTH

17ᵀᴴ CENTURY
c.1692

RJS 1995

(12)

EXTANT FEATURES.
F PREHISTORIC FORDING PLACE.
C ROMAN CROSSING PLACE.
W WELL
S STONE

— · · — · · PREHISTORIC TRACKWAY.
— · · · — POSSIBLE PREHISTORIC TRACKWAY.
—————— ROMAN.
— — — — POSSIBLE ROMAN.
— · — · — SAXON.
· · · · · · POSSIBLE SAXON.
········· 1066 TO 1700.
·········· WAY DENIED TO VILLAGERS,
           POSSIBLE FOOT PATH OR
— ·· — ·· RELEGATE TO F.P.
— ··· — ··· OLD TRACK BECOMING
           DISUSED c.1700 ONWARD.
           c.1700 ONWARD.

1000 m
1000 yards
0   km   1
0 miles 1

46

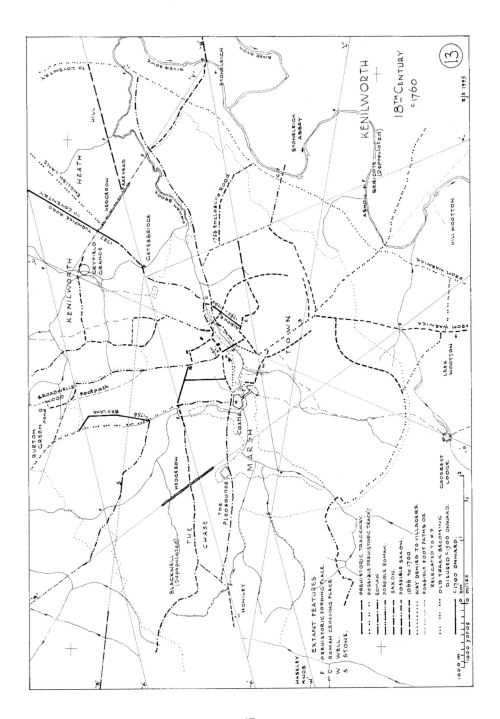

KENILWORTH
18TH CENTURY.
c1760

13

R/S 1995

EXTANT FEATURES.
F PREHISTORIC FORDING PLACE.
C ROMAN CROSSING PLACE.
W WELL.
S STONE.

––– – –– PREHISTORIC TRACKWAY.
····· –··· POSSIBLE PREHISTORIC TRACK.
–·–·–·– ROMAN.
––·––·–– POSSIBLE ROMAN.
–– –– –– SAXON.
············ POSSIBLE SAXON.
–––––––– 1066 TO 1700.
·········· WAY DENIED TO VILLAGERS.
·········· POSSIBLE FOOT PATHS OR RELEGATED TO F.P.
··· ···· OLD TRACK BECOMING DISUSED c.1700 ONWARD.
············ c.1700 ONWARD.

1000 m
0   km   1   2
1000 yards
0 miles

TO COVENTRY
RIVER SOWE
STONELEIGH
RIVER AVON
STONELEIGH ABBEY
ASHOW
BERICOTE (Depopulated)
HILL WOOTTON
FROM WARWICK
FROM WARWICK
LEEK WOOTTON
GOODREST LODGE
HILL
HEATH
ENGLISH LANE
1721 TURNPIKE ROAD TO COVENTRY
AXEHEAD
HEDGEROW
FINHAM BROOK
CATTESBRIDGE
GRYFIELD GRANGE
KENILWORTH
1756 Enclosure Road
TOWN
Castle
The Pleasaunce
MARSH
CHASE
HEDGEROW
THE
RED LANE c1756
Footpath
BROADWELL WOOD
Pond
BURTON GREEN
BLACKWELL (Depopulated)
HONILEY
HASELEY KNOB
47

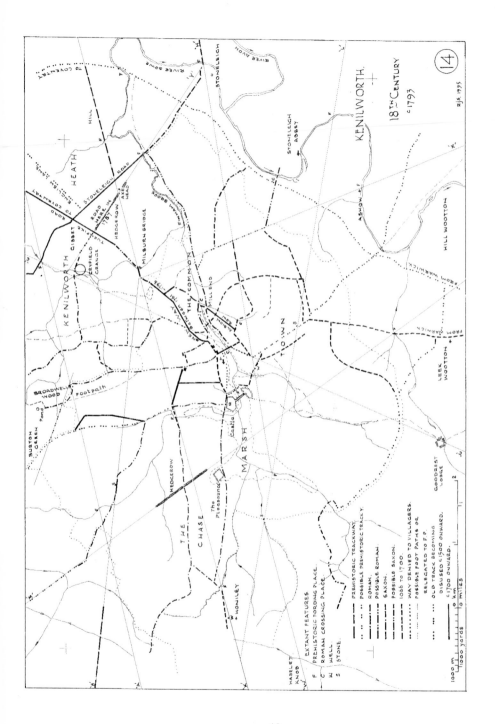

KENILWORTH.

18TH CENTURY
c 1793

RJS 1995

(14)

EXTANT FEATURES
F PREHISTORIC FORDING PLACE.
C ROMAN CROSSING PLACE.
W WELL.
S STONE.

PREHISTORIC TRACKWAY.
POSSIBLE PREHISTORIC TRACK.
ROMAN.
POSSIBLE ROMAN.
SAXON.
POSSIBLE SAXON.
1066 TO 1700.
WAY DENIED TO VILLAGERS.
POSSIBLE FOOT PATHS OR
RELEGATED TO F.P.
OLD TRACK BECOMING
DISUSED c 1700 ONWARD.
c 1700 ONWARD.

1000 M
1000 yards
km
miles